Gary Jones

Copenhagen

First published by Gary Jones in 2016

Copyright © Gary Jones, 2016

All rights reserved. No part of this publication may be reproduced, stored, or transmitted in any form or by any means, electronic, mechanical, photocopying, recording, scanning, or otherwise without written permission from the publisher. It is illegal to copy this book, post it to a website, or distribute it by any other means without permission.

This book was professionally typeset on Reedsy. Find out more at reedsy.com

Contents

Introduction	1
A Brief History of Copenhagen	3
Transport and Safety	6
Areas of Copenhagen	10
So when is the best time to visit Copenhagen?	18
The Best Museums in the City	20
The Best Art Galleries	24
The Best Coffee Shops in Copenhagen	30
The Best Bars and Night Clubs	36
Top 4 Affordable Hotels	40
Restaurants	43
Special Things to Do only in Copenhagen	47
3-Day Itinerary	53
Conclusion	57

1

Introduction

Before heading out to Copenhagen, you should arm yourself with useful information. This book provides you with all the things you need to know about this beautiful city.

Here are a few things you can learn through this travel guide:

-Discover how this beautiful city came to be by exploring its history briefly

-Travel like a local by learning which public transportation to take at which time

-Learn about each neighborhood and what they have to offer

-Find out when the best time to pay Copenhagen a visit is

-Discover more about the city's rich history with our list of best museums

-Explore the art and culture of Copenhageners from their exquisite displays in the best art galleries

-Find out where to get the best coffee in the city

-Let the Copenhageners show you how to party with our list of best bars and nightclubs

-Book a superb accommodation at affordable prices with our list of budget friendly hotels

-Have a unique gastronomic experience like no other with Copenhagen's best restaurants

-Have an unforgettable experience doing special things that can only be done in Copenhagen

Also included is a sample 3-day itinerary to make your trip pleasant and organized.

Thanks again for downloading this book, I hope you enjoy it!

2

A Brief History of Copenhagen

A Brief History of Copenhagen
The biggest Scandinavian city and the capital of Denmark, Copenhagen is a busy business hub and center for the arts and culture. The city offers plenty of entertainment options. It is also known as a culinary hotspot, offering a unique gastronomic experience.

Copenhagen was built!

Copenhagen was founded in 1167 by King Valdemar I's counsellor, Bishop Absalon. Valdemar the Great tasked Absalon to build the city in an effort to protect the trade. The first fortress was built on the isle of Slotsholmen. The original castle of Absalon has now become the foundation of the Christianborg Palace.

Because of its ideal location for harbor, Copenhagen rose from a simple fishing village to a respectable city in the 12th century. In 1443, Copenhagen became the Danish capital, replacing Roskilde.

The first King of Denmark was crowned in Copenhagen in 1449, King Christian I. He founded the first university in Denmark, the historical Copenhagen University.

The Reformation Era

In 1536, the Protestant Reformation came to Copenhagen and Denmark. With the initiative of King Christian III who ruled in 1503 to 1559, the Protestant movement was introduced in the country. It marked the reformation of the Danish Church. Today, 90 percent of Danes are members of the Evangelian-Lutheran Church.

The Architect of Copenhagen

From 1588 to 1648, a ruler known as the great builder and architect of Copenhagen by the name of King Christian IV reigned. During his reign, plenty of remarkable projects and building were constructed. The first and now the world's oldest amusement park, the Bakken, was built during his time. The Old Citadel, which protected the city against England in the Battle of Copenhagen in 1807, was also built under King Christian IV's rule. Other notable projects that still stand today include the Round Tower built in 1642, the Old Stock Exchange built in 1620 and the Rosenborg Castle in 1634.

When King Christian IV died at the age of 70 in 1648, King Frederik III was crowned. He continued the works of his predecessor and went on to build the Royal Library. The Royal Danish Guards were also established under his rule.

Copenhagen in the 18th Century

The economy and trade continued to grow in the 18th century. Unfortunately, Copenhagen witnessed and suffered plenty of misfortunes during this time. In 1711, the Bubonic plague wiped out close to a third of the population. In 1728, fires ruined and heavily damaged the city. The Copenhageners were quick to recover, however. In 1737, reconstruction and rebuilding of the city was completed.

The first newspaper of Copenhagen, the Royal Danish Theatre, the first free hospital and the Royal Danish Porcelain factory were all established. It would seem that Copenhagen was back on its feet. Unfortunately, Copenhagen was attacked by the British with their heavy bombs. The city suffered in casualties and destruction from 1801 to 1807.

The spirit of the Danish people was rekindled in 1808. The year marked the tradition of Christmas celebration in the city. it also paved the way to unite the Danish Christian culture.

Denmark went bankrupt in 1813. The economy eventually recovered over the years and still going strong today as evident in modern Copenhagen.

3

Transport and Safety

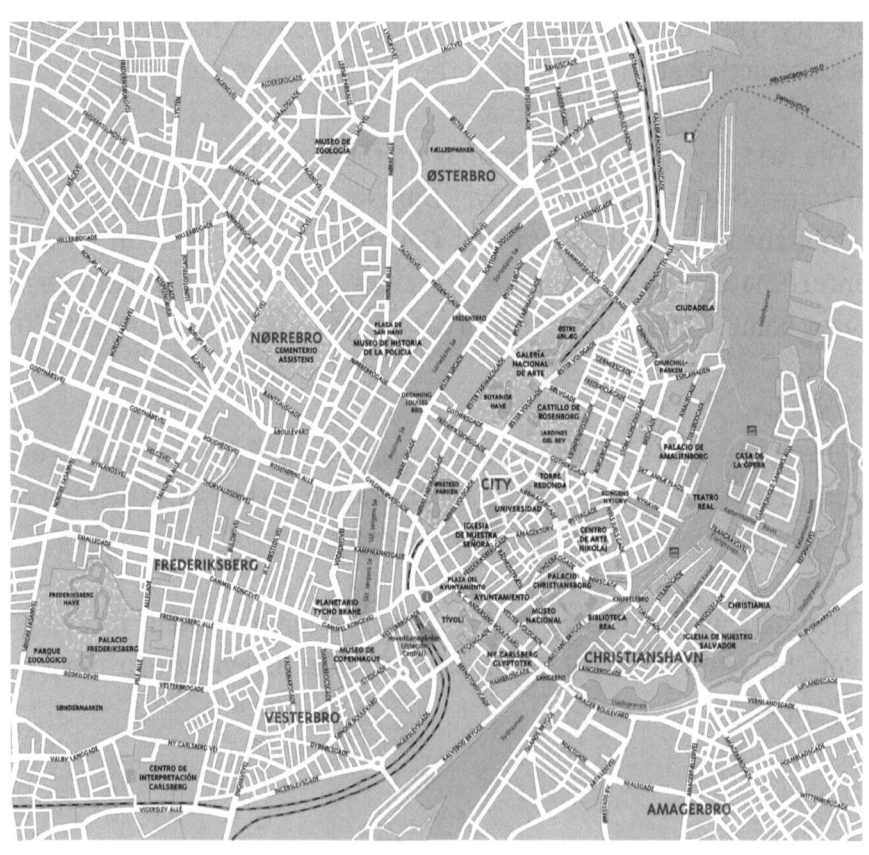

Getting Into The City
If you are flying into Copenhagen, you will arrive at Copenhagen Airport, Kastrup. You will have many transport options to get into the city. You can get into the city by subway, train, bus or taxi.

Phone: +45 32 31 32 31 (airport)
Airport Website
https://www.cph.dk/en/
Airport Map
https://goo.gl/maps/zB88rc4WqQw

Getting around Copenhagen is easy and simple. That's because you can access the trains, Metro, buses and waterbuses using the same ticket. The public transport is also reliable and punctual. Here is a list of the transports that can take you around the city.

Copenhagen Card
A good option for cheap travel is the Copenhagen Card that will give you many benefits including the following:
  -Free admission to 74 museums and attractions.
  -Free transport by train, bus, harbour bus and Subway in the entire Copenhagen Region – also from and to the airport.
  -Discounts on car hire, restaurants and sights.
Copenhagen Card Website
http://www.copenhagencard.com/whats-included

By Bus
Copenhagen's primary buses are called A-buses. They will take you around the city center. They are open to serve the public at all hours. You can cut your travel time by taking the S-buses because they have fewer stops. Rush hour is between 7 and 9 in the morning and 3:30 to 5:30 in the afternoon.
Bus Website
http://www.dsb.dk/en

By Metro
Copenhagen's Metro is available 24/7.
Metro Website
http://www.dsb.dk/en

By Train
There are different lines depending on the route. The S-trains are open from 5am to 12:30 at night. Lines A, B, C and E run every 10 minutes while lines H and Bx every 20 minutes. Line F runs every 4 minutes.

If you want a slow tour of the city, you can also take a boat ride by the canal.

Train Website
http://www.dsb.dk/en

Bicycles

When in Copenhagen you should rent a bike and explore the city. The people of Copenhagen are known for their love of riding bikes. It is biking heaven in Copenhagen. The city has over 390 kilometers of designated bike lanes.

Bicycles Rental Website
http://copenhagenbicycles.dk/rent/
Bicycles Rental Map
https://goo.gl/maps/XVVUkARAZY62

Safety in Copenhagen

This is generally a safe city. However, just like other busy cities, you need to take precautions during your stay.

Be wary of pickpockets especially around the central station. Thieves also abound in the busy pedestrian street of Strøget and around the City Hall Square. Some tourists have been scammed by individuals posing as police officers. If you are approached by a police officer, ask for legitimate identification. The Copenhagen police will not ask you to pay fines on the spot for breaking a law.

The Copenhagen police can be contacted at 114. During emergency situations, call 112.

4

Areas of Copenhagen

Copenhagen has plenty of interesting sights to see and things to experience. The following are the different areas in the city and the best they could offer to tourists.

Tivoli Gardens

Built in 1843, Tivoli Gardens is found in the south of Rådhuspladsen. These amusement gardens have a fantastic lineup of theaters, dance halls, restaurants and beer gardens. This is where you will see exotic flowers. Tivoli has about 160,000 of them. It is beautifully adorned with 110,000 electric lights. It is also surrounded by beautiful lakes that further contribute to its serene and fairy tale atmosphere. The Tivoli Gardens is one of the many reasons why thousands of tourists visit Copenhagen each year.

In addition to the lush gardens and charming architecture, Tivoli also offers magical rides. Among the most famous is the Vertigo which is an thrilling ride that turns upside down at a speed of 100 km/h. It was actually named Europe's Best Ride in 2014. Another popular ride is the wooden Roller Coaster built in 1914. It's an old school roller coaster with a brakeman on board that mans each train.

The Tivoli Gardens is most crowded during the summer but the amusement park also holds special events throughout the year. It is highly recommended whether you are travelling with your kids or on a romantic vacation.

Tivoli Gardens Website
https://www.tivoli.dk/en/
Tivoli Gardens Map
https://goo.gl/maps/SMr7M6zGjg22

Strøget

Strøget consists of 5 interconnected streets: Østergade, Amagertorv, Villelskaftet, Nygade and Frederiksberggade. This is where you will find two of Copenhagen's busiest plazas, the Kongens Nytorv and the Rådhuspladsen. Also found in this area are two smaller squares which are equally spectacular, the Nytorv and Gammeltorv. These squares come alive during the summer with plenty of outdoor seating outside its marvelous lineup of restaurants.

Strøget Map
https://goo.gl/maps/vMbBCqi3hwE2

Nyhavn or Kongens Nytorv

Nyhavn means "New Harbor." Originally built in 1670, Nyhavn provided shelter for sailors during storms. It was also a place here sailors used to stop by for cheap drinks, tattoos and other kinds of diversions. Today, some of the antique fishing boats are still here which gives the area an old fashion charm. It has an exciting lineup of restaurants. In fact, it houses most of Copenhagen's best restaurants.

There are outdoor terraces as well which are usually filled on holidays when the Danes like to chatter

and drink hard. Above the Nyhavn canal, the King's New Market or Kongens Nytorv is found where the Royal Theater and the deluxe Hotel

d'Angleterre are located.
Nyhavn or Kongens Nytorv Map
https://goo.gl/maps/UQ3HRCEmfw62

Indre By
Found at the heart of Copenhagen, Indre By is a beautiful Old Town. The neighborhood once consisted of monasteries, beautiful squares and a maze of alley ways and streets. Today, you will find charming buildings that links to the university. The Round Tower or Rundetårn and the Cathedral of Copenhagen or Vor Frue Kirke can be found in this area.
Indre By Map
https://goo.gl/maps/7NVrRWieuV42

Slotsholmen
In this side of Copenhagen lies the Christiansborg Palace which was where the first fortress was built by Bishop Absalon in 1167. Today, this island is home to the Thorvaldsen's Museum, the Danish parliament, the Royal Library, the Royal Museum and the Theatre Museum. You will also find the 17th-century Børsen or stock exchange here. You can get here by taking the bridge that links Indre By to this neighborhood.
Slotsholmen Map
https://goo.gl/maps/aXup7MA6MPS2

Christianshavn
Originally built according to the Dutch Renaissance style mainly for workers of the shipbuilding industry, this "new town" of the 1500's has seen many changes. Today, it is most popular for its attractions including the Vors Frelsers Kirke and the Danish Film Museum. The spire of the church provides a steep climb where visitors can marvel at the beautiful panoramic view of the city.

This area also houses the free city of Christiana which used serve as barracks for soldiers and home to the youth and homeless people. Today, restaurants and craft shops can be found near Christiana in the Prinsessegade area. The prices of food and goods here are quite cheap simply because the residents do not want to pay 25% sales tax.
Christianshavn Map
https://goo.gl/maps/aRNqScGkV332

Vesterbro
What used to be a slum for prostitutes and junkies has now become a place where Copenhagen's hippest bars, cafes and ethnic restaurants are found. People come here to party and experience cultural diversity. Although Vesterbro does not have famous museums and monuments, it does have plenty of other things to offer like food markets, ethnic gift shops and even sex shops.
Vesterbro Map
https://goo.gl/maps/WfhVXac99xT2

Nørrebro
Found right next to Vesterbro is Nørrebro where immigrants abound.

This neighborhood is overflowing with ethnic restaurants and artisan shops, mostly Pakistani and Turkish. There are antique shops everywhere too especially along Ravnsborgade.

Nørrebro also houses the Assistens Kirkegård, Copenhagen's historic cemetery where the remains of Søren Kierkegaard and Hans Christian Andersen lay rest. Nørrebro also has an exciting night scene. The best nightlife hotspots in the city are found in Blågårdsgade and Sankt Hans Torv.

Nørrebro Map
https://goo.gl/maps/LKVu8z5EWc62

Frederiksberg

This is both a business and residential district. Its focal point is the Frederiksberg Palace with a rich Italian style and a charming ocher facade. The surrounding area is a park called the Frederiksberg Have. To the west is the Zoologisk Have, one of Europe's largest zoos.

Frederiksberg Map
https://goo.gl/maps/vQbJ2kLV6t82

Dragør

This 16th century fishing village is now a favorite leisure spot in

Copenhagen. Dragør boasts of national landmarks including the 65 old red-roofed houses and cobblestone streets. It is a superb representation of 18th-century Danish village.
 Dragør Map
 https://goo.gl/maps/hgvFUAU5QWt

5

So when is the best time to visit Copenhagen?

The weather is loveliest during the summer, that's between May and September. During the warm months, the streets are alive, the cafés and restaurants set up outdoor seating where guests can enjoy the lovely breeze. The summer months also have plenty to offer when it comes to festivals and other events.

When October comes, the festivals are over and Copenhagen prepares for the harsh winter. In December, the mood becomes festive and preparations are made for the holiday celebrations.

It is best to visit Copenhagen between June and August. Among the key events these times of the year include the Copenhagen Jazz Festival, Roskilde Festival and the Little Mermaid's Birthday. The downside is your trip will be a little more expensive. Because of the heavy influx of tourists, hotel accommodations and other expenses are higher.

From September to November, the weather becomes a little more frigid. The upside is that it is much less expensive to travel and stay at Copenhagen during the autumn. Plus, there are a few events you can still join and enjoy during your stay including the Copenhagen Blues Festival in September and Copenhagen Night of Culture in October.

March and May mark the spring time. The spring weather in Copenhagen is not as lovely as the summer. It is friendly and tolerable nevertheless. The best news is there are fewer crowds. Airfare and accommodations are also much lower. Tivoli Gardens is open by this time of the year. Notable Spring events include the Copenhagen Puppet Festival, the Copenhagen Beer Festival and the Copenhagen Carnival.

If your vacation budget allows it, you might as well go during the summer. Otherwise, you can go in spring or autumn.

6

The Best Museums in the City

The city of Copenhagen has many stories to tell. From the ancient palaces and castles to the narrow and cobblestone streets, everything speaks of its rich history. Learn more about the city from the Stone Age to the 20th century through the following best museums Copenhagen has to offer.

The National Museum
Housed in The Prince's Palace, the National Museum in itself along with its ornate pieces of furniture and elegant halls are part of rich history. Among the things that can be seen here are exhibitions of Danish history from the Stone Age to the Viking age to the middle ages to the Renaissance and Modern ages. Other notable things to see include the extensive ethnographical collection from coins to medals and toys.

The Danish antiquity that feature national treasures including the archeological discoveries that date back to the Viking Age, the Bronze Age Egtved Girl and the Sun Chariot, which is more than 3,000 years old. The remains of the Huldremose Woman from the first decade of the first century are also on display in this museum. Kids can have fun admiring history through the Children's Museum. There are English self-guided tours as well. The museum is open from Tuesdays to Sundays at 10am to 5am on February to December. Admission is free.

Address: Prince's Mansion, Ny Vestergade 10, 1471
The National Museum Website
http://en.natmus.dk/
The National Museum Map
https://goo.gl/maps/nWTKVVrYq3M2

The Museum of National History

The Frederiksborg Castle was burned down to the ground in 1859. It was rebuilt and restored as a museum in 1878. Also known as the Frederiksborg Museum, the National Historic Museum features historical paintings, portraits, furniture and other art works that speak of Denmark's history from the introduction of Christianity to the modern era.

You can visit this museum from Monday to Sundays between 10am to 5pm on April to October and between 11am to 3pm on November to March. The admission fee for adults is 75.00 DKK. Children from 6 to 15 years old are admitted for 20.00 DKK.

Address: 3400 Hillerød
The Museum of National History Website
http://www.dnm.dk/dk/index.htm
The Museum of National History Map
https://goo.gl/maps/MgMMdxsj2332

The Royal Danish Naval Museum

If you're interested in naval history, this is a must-see museum. The Royal Danish Naval Museum boasts of an extensive historic naval model collection including submarine interiors, uniforms, nautical instruments, marine paintings, ship decorations and naval artillery. It is a thrilling experience that gives you the opportunity to get up close and personal to more than 400 ship models on display that represent the shipbuilding development that has occurred over the past 300 years.

Children can have an exciting tour as they are given the opportunity to board a reconstruction of the Danish warship. Admission is free. The museum is open from Tuesday to Sunday between 12nn to 4pm on May to December.

Address: Overgaden Oven Vandet 58, 1415
The Royal Danish Naval Museum Website
http://natmus.dk/museerne/orlogsmuseet/
The Royal Danish Naval Museum Map
https://goo.gl/maps/sQzLWGczz6u

Thorvaldsen's Museum

Bertel Thorvaldsen, a renowned Danish sculptor in the 1800s donated his art collection to Copenhagen, his native city. His large collection is housed in one of Copenhagen's finest buildings designed by M.B. Bindesbøll and built from 1839 to 1848. This museum is home to Thorvaldsen's sculpture masterpieces. His antique and painting collections are also on display.

The museum is open from Tuesdays to Sundays from 10am to 5pm on January to December. Admission fee for adults is 40.00 DKK. Admission for visitors below 18 years of age is free.

Address:Bertel Thorvaldsens Plads 2, 1213
Thorvaldsen's Museum Website
http://www.thorvaldsensmuseum.dk/en
Thorvaldsen's Museum Map
https://goo.gl/maps/A4VZxJ9wbRy

The Workers' Museum
Are you curious about how average Copenhageners lived in the 50's? This museum shows you just how. The Workers' Museum recounts stories of working class families including that of the Sørensen family. Visitors get the chance to taste what was popular in those days including the kiksekage, a rich cracker cake and the wartime coffee substitute. The museum has a dedicated area for 20th century homes and shops called the People's Century Lane.

The museum is open every day between 10am and 4pm. Admission for adults is 65.00 DKK. Admission is free for visitors under the age of 18 years.

Address:Rømersgade 22, 1362
The Workers' Museum Website
http://www.arbejdermuseet.dk/
The Workers' Museum Map
https://goo.gl/maps/MyUYoLa9Nzn

7

The Best Art Galleries

Along with its rich history, Copenhagen is also a haven for the arts. If you are a fan of art, you can explore the Danish and international art scene from the Golden Age to the contemporary era in these beautiful galleries.

The National Gallery of Denmark

This is the largest art museum in Denmark featuring exquisite art from Danish and other artists from the past 700 years. There are Renaissance classics as well as modern and contemporary art. The most popular is the beautiful art collection from the Danish Golden Age. The gallery boasts of Matisse's best collections.

The National Gallery of Denmark holds several art-based events throughout the year where visitors can join in art talks and music while enjoying food and drinks. The Royal Cast Collection which features more than 2000 plaster sculptures representing over 4000 years of history about Christian tales and pagan gods is also a part of the gallery.

The gallery offers guided tours and workshop activities. Children and families can join in the drawing room and exhibitions to explore their inner creativity.

The museum is open on Tuesdays, Thursdays to Sundays from 10am to 5pm on January to December. They are also open on Wednesdays between 10am and 8pm. Admission is free on the permanent exhibitions. Adult admission fee for special exhibitions is at 110.00 DKK and 85.00 DKK for young adults.

Address:Sølvgade 48-50, 1307
The National Gallery of Denmark Website
http://www.smk.dk/en/
The National Gallery of Denmark Map
https://goo.gl/maps/ob3SD7SiKMv

The Hirschsprung Collection

19th and early 20th century Danish art is represented well in this gallery. The Hirschsprung Collection features art works from the Danish Golden Age to the Skagen and all the way to Modern Breakthrough. Masterpieces from Hammershøi, Krøyer, Købke and Eckersberg are on display.

The beautiful collection is housed in a stunning neo-classical style building of special importance located in central Copenhagen. A tobacco manufacturer by the name of Heinrich Hirschsprung donated his personal art collection in 1902 to the Danish state. The gallery is designed and built around his collection where it is now enjoyed by the Danes and visitors from all over the world.

The gallery is open from Tuesdays to Sundays between 11am to 4pm from November to December. Admission fee for adults is at 75.00 DKK and free for visitors under 18 years old. On Wednesdays, entrance is free for everyone.

Address:Stockholmsgade 20, 2100

The Hirschsprung Collection Website
http://www.hirschsprung.dk/default.aspx
The Hirschsprung Collection Map
https://goo.gl/maps/P9vgPGg7ARm

Glyptoteket
Founded by the renowned brewer, Carl Jacobsen in 1888, Glyptoteket consists of two departments: the ancient and modern art. The gallery has an extensive display of exquisite artwork, and the architectural surroundings is just as stunning.

In the Department of Antiquities, visitors will find fine collections of artworks from Egyptians, Greeks, Etruscans and Romans. It will take you to 3500 years of history and art.

The Modern Department, on the other hand, features sculptures and paintings from the 19th to 20th centuries from Danish and French artists. Among the things that Glyptoteket boasts of are the 35 sculptures by Rodin, Degas' complete series of bronzes, 40+ works by Gauguin along with the finest works from the Denmark's Golden Age and French Impressionism. Glyptoteket also holds special exhibitions to enhance the public's art experience.

The gallery is open on Tuesdays, Wednesdays and Friday to Sundays between 11am and 6pm from March to December. They are also open on Thursdays from 11am to 10pm. The admission fee for adults is 95.00 DKK and free for visitors under 18 years old.

Address:Dantes Plads 7, 1556
Glyptoteket Website
http://www.glyptoteket.com/
Glyptoteket Map
https://goo.gl/maps/mrYLcySt8632

Kunsthal Charlottenborg

One of Europe's largest contemporary art spaces, Kunsthal Charlottenborg has a strong international focus. It has plenty of events and exhibitions with screenings, talks and performances all in an effort to reach a wider range of audiences. The art space mounts 3 seasons annually. It is known in Copenhagen as a true champion of contemporary art.

The gallery is open on Wednesdays between 11am and 8pm on May to December. It also opens from Tuesdays to Sundays 11am to 5pm throughout the months of May. Admission fee for adults us 60.00 DKK and free for visitors below 16 years old.

Address:Nyhavn 2, 1051
Kunsthal Charlottenborg Website
http://www.charlottenborg.dk/forside?lang=eng
Kunsthal Charlottenborg Map
https://goo.gl/maps/CBzCfYbPnSM2

Den Frie Centre of Contemporary Art

The gallery has a long standing tradition of supporting contemporary art and architecture. Houses in a wooden building designed by J.F. Willumsen and founded in 1898, Den Frie prides itself as a house of artists, envisioning the art of the future.

The gallery is open on Tuesdays, Wednesdays, and Friday to Sundays between 12nn and 6pm from January to December. It also opens on Thursdays from 12nn to 9pm. The admission fee for adults is 60.00 DKK and free for visitors below 12 years old.

Address:Oslo Pl. 1, 2100
Den Frie Centre of Contemporary Art Website
http://en.denfrie.dk/

Den Frie Centre of Contemporary Art Map
https://goo.gl/maps/kNAriJbuyz12

8

The Best Coffee Shops in Copenhagen

Copenhagen does not fall short when it comes to great quality coffee. Because of the cold weather, the Copenhageners appreciate excellent coffee and there are plenty of shops that serve a good cup around the city. Here are a couple of coffee shops you should try while you're in the city.

Kent Kaffe Laboratorium

Located in the neighborhood of Indre By along Nørre Farimagsgade, Kent Kaffe Laboratorium offers a unique experience for coffee lovers. They are most known for their classics as well as their impressively advanced brewing methods. The coffee beans they use are 100 percent organic, imported from different parts of the world.

As the name suggests, the interior is laboratory inspired. Customers are encouraged to experiment with their coffee. You can even have yours in a flask brewed over a bunsen burner. Kent Kaffe Laboratorium serves a wide range of breads and cakes including the organic face sandwich the Copenhageners call smørrebrød.

This coffee shop is open from Monday to Friday between 9am and 5:30pm. It also opens on Saturdays from 11am to 5pm and on Sundays from 12nn to 5pm.

Address: Nørre Farimagsgade 70, 1364
Kent Kaffe Laboratorium Website
http://www.kentkaffelaboratorium.com/
Kent Kaffe Laboratorium Map
https://goo.gl/maps/8DyqHryepeB2

The Coffee Collective, Jægersborggade

The Coffee Collective is more than just a coffee shop. They are making a great effort to provide extraordinary coffee experience by paying much attention to the coffee making process. In cooperation with farmers, The Coffee Collective aims to develop a more sustainable way of producing and improving coffee quality. You will experience the difference when you taste their great coffee.

The coffee shop is open to serve great coffee on Mondays to Fridays from 7am to 7pm on July to December. They are also open on the weekends from 8am to 7pm.

At Jægersborggade, the atmosphere is relaxing and the baristas are welcoming. The Coffee Collective also has to other shops located in Gothåbsvej and Torvehallerne.

Address: Jægersborggade 10, 2200
The Coffee Collective, Jægersborggade Website
http://coffeecollective.dk/
The Coffee Collective, Jægersborggade Map
https://goo.gl/maps/wVFWNoqCij92

Coffee First
Used to be Estate Coffee, Coffee First is a rather small coffee shop located across the street from the lakes and the Planetarium. People come here for a taste of their unbeatable estate coffee. Another must try from this place are their delicious chocolate desserts that hail from Strangas. They also serve breakfast plates at DKK 79.

This coffee shop located along Gammel Kongevej is open on weekdays of March to December between 7:30am and 8pm. On weekends, they are open from 10am to 8pm.

Address: Gammel Kongevej 1, 1610
Coffee First Website
https://sites.google.com/site/wwwcoffeefirstdk/
Coffee First Map
https://goo.gl/maps/TCPftDWEcpN2

Parterre
Found in the maritime Christianshavn district, Parterre is a newly established coffee shop that has quickly earned an excellent reputation. This basement coffee has a rustic feel to it but with the lights and the beautiful decorations, the shop has a unique appeal. In fact, customers like to take pictures in the café.

This coffee shop in Indre By along Ovengaden Oven Vandet serves coffee on weekdays between 7am and 6pm. They are also open on weekends from 9am to 6pm. They are open to serve throughout the year.

More than the nice interior however, people stop by the Parterre for the excellent coffee that comes from the Koppi, a Swedish roaster. For a good cup of coffee, the prices at Parterre are very reasonable. A coffee cup will only cost you between 26.00 and 36.00 DKK

Breakfast and lunch plates are also available. You can also have some delicious cake slices to enjoy with your coffee.

Address: Overgaden Oven Vandet 90, 1415
Parterre Website
https://goo.gl/hG1hFy
Parterre Map
https://goo.gl/maps/owbxfNBWmg32

Kafferiet
If you want variety, you can head to the Kafferiet at Esplanaden. They serve 15 different types of coffee. They also offer iced coffee, smoothies, tea, sandwiches, muffins and croissants. You can order coffee to go and stroll around the Citadel too. Or you can buy five different kinds of coffee beans from them so you can make some at home.

Found along Esplanaden, Kafferiet serves coffee on weekdays from 7:30am to 6pm and on weekends from 10am to 6pm all year round.

Address: Esplanaden 44, 1263
Kafferiet Website
https://goo.gl/exc1lO

Kafferiet Map
https://goo.gl/maps/VnNbzSeiaJJ2

Risteriet, Studiestræde

Located along the lively street of Studiestræde, Risteriet offers a great selection of coffee beans. You can buy aromatic beans from them or some coffee equipment. They also sell green coffee beans if you fancy roasting some yourself.

If you don't want to go through all the trouble of making coffee for yourself, you can have a cup at Risteriet and enjoy it from the outside seating where you can bask at a nice view of the streets. Risteriet has another shop located at the Vesterbro neighborhood along Halmtorvet.

Located in the neighborhood of Indre By, Risteriet is open on weekends from 8am to 6pm, on Saturdays from 10am to 5pm and on Sundays from 10am to 3pm throughout the year.

Address: Studiestræde 36, 1455
Risteriet, Studiestræde Website
http://www.risteriet.dk/
Risteriet, Studiestræde Map
https://goo.gl/maps/Pm1ezdZxf692

Original Coffee

Nothing beats a good coffee taht you can enjoy around a cosy atmosphere. That is exactly what the Original Coffee offers. They serve high quality coffee with a great variety. The beans are locally roasted. They also offer Irish Coffees as well as sandwiches and decadent cakes that come from an organic bakery.

A minimalistic style interior, Original Coffee provides a safe haven for their customers where they can enjoy their coffee in a stress-free environment. Original Coffee has three more shops located at Bredgade, Strandvejen and Trianglen. The shop at Nordre Frihavnsgade in Trianglen has a great view of the lake. It was in fact, voted as the best coffee shop in Copenhagen of 2013.

Address: Østergade 52, 1001
Original Coffee
https://www.facebook.com/originalcoffee/
Original Coffee
https://goo.gl/maps/oQkTBcHRukF2

Café Glyptoteket

Glyptoteket is not only a place of art. It is also a place for a relaxing cup of coffee. Another beautiful sight at the art museum is the beautiful winter garden where Café Glyptoteket is found. The café serves coffee, sumptuous cakes and homemade Danish lunch dishes. The owners use sustainable and organic ingredients. Relax with a cup of coffee at hand as you enjoy every sip surrounded by exotic flowers, plants and palm trees.

Café Glyptoteket is open from Tuesdays to Sundays between 11am and 5pm throughout December. Prices of dishes range between DKK 95 and DKK 200.

Address: Dantes Plads 7, 1556
Café Glyptoteket Website
http://www.glyptoteket.dk/besoeg/cafe
Café Glyptoteket Map
https://goo.gl/maps/jK9Usgaa5fz

9

The Best Bars and Night Clubs

Copenhageners know how to have a great time. It shows with their excellent line up of bars and clubs that guarantees a night of fun. If you like to party or simply have a drink or two before heading to your hotel, check out these cool spots in Copenhagen.

WarPigs
Serving 22 quality taps, WarPigs is very well known for providing an

extraordinary beer experience. Expect nothing less from this brewpub established by two big names in the brewery scene, American brewery 3 Floyds and Danish brewer Mikkeller. They have an on-site brewery. They do not only offer freshly made craft beer, WarPigs also serve authentic Texas barbecue.

Address: Flæsketorvet 25, 1117 København K
Phone: +45 4348 4848
WarPigs Website
http://warpigs.dk/
WarPigs Map
https://goo.gl/maps/uiRJt1UY2Zv

Mikkeler Bar
Established by no other than the world famous brewer Mikkel Borg Bjergsø in 2007, Mikkeler Bar is known for offering 10 taps from Mikkeler itself and 5 others from world's best breweries. They also serve the best snacks and cheese. Specialized bottled selections are also available.

The bar is open to serve on Mondays to Wednesdays and Sundays from 1pm to 1am, on Thursdays to Fridays from 1pm to 2am and on Saturdays between 12nn and 2am on October to December. Check out Mikkeler and Friends at Copenhagen's Nørrebro area too.

Address: Victoriagade 8 B-C, 1655 København V
Phone: +45 33310415
Mikkeler Website
http://mikkeller.dk/location/mikkeller-bar-aarhus/
Mikkeler Map
https://goo.gl/maps/GrMgwSgA5oo

1105

Known as a trendy bar for the 30-something, 1105 serves magical potions in the form of topnotch cocktails. The atmosphere is modern and chic. The bar also serves modern shakes and classic cocktails. A must-try is the Copenhagen cocktail, an original creation of 1105's cocktail tender, Gromit.

The cocktail bar is open on Fridays from 4pm to 2am, on Wednesdays, Thursdays and Saturdays between 8pm and 2am all year round.

Address: Kristen Bernikows Gade 4, 1105 København K
Phone: +45 3393 1105
1105 Website
http://www.1105.dk/
1105 Map
https://goo.gl/maps/XuWWixvyaot

HIVE
An exclusive club found near Gammeltorv, Hive always has something exciting in store for party hungry peeps. On Fridays, Hive caters to an energetic audience. The club ensures the music doesn't stop with their excellent DJ lineup. On Saturdays, Hive completely transforms itself playing mixes from the 1300s complete with dungeons along with 3-dimensional visuals.

The club is only open on Fridays and Saturdays between 11pm and 5am from January to December. If you happen to check them out though, you are guaranteed to have a fun, unforgettable evening.

Address: Skindergade 45-47, 1159 København K
Phone: +45 2845 7467
HIVE Website
https://goo.gl/oXPjms
HIVE Map

https://goo.gl/maps/wcf63CN1en92

Culture Box

If you are a huge fan of electronic music, Culture Box is the place to be. This is one of Denmark's most prominent nightclubs. It is known for bringing together underground local artists and also an impressive line-up of international artists. The club consists of three compartments.

The White Box is designed as a pre-clubbing bar. The Red Box provides a more intimate atmosphere located in the lower floor and the Black Box is built with a massive sound system where guests can check out some of the biggest names in the music scene.

Culture Box plays a mix of electronica, house, techno and bass music. They are open on Fridays and Saturdays from 11pm onwards throughout the year. The admission fee ranges between 50.00 DKK and 100.00 DKK.

Address: Kronprinsessegade 54 St., 1306 København K
Phone: +45 3332 5050
Culture Box Website
http://www.culture-box.com/
Culture Box Map
https://goo.gl/maps/44GJSmq8jq32

10

Top 4 Affordable Hotels

You don't have to spend a lot on accommodation. There are plenty of excellent but inexpensive hotels in Copenhagen. These 4 are at the top of the list.

Wake Up Copenhagen
Planted in a central location, Wake Up is found in the south side of Copenhagen's main train station. It's not the quietest. The surrounding is slightly industrial. Although it's a budget hotel, its compact rooms are impressively designed according to slick Scandinavian style complete with modern amenities. The rate for standard double rooms starts at £60. If you can spare extra £25-35 a night, you can get a room on the top floor that gives you a stunning view of the city.

Address: Carsten Niebuhrs Gade 11, 1577
Phone:+45 4480 0000
Wake Up Copenhagen Website
https://www.wakeupcopenhagen.com/#/search
Wake Up Copenhagen Map
https://goo.gl/maps/i1UMxwPxrBL2

Hotel Sct Thomas
There's an area in Copenhagen fondly called small Paris. It's in Værndedamsvej which is a street found in between Frederiksberg and

Vesterbro. Værndedamsvej is a nice area in Copenhagen because it has an array of food shops, bars, and restaurants. The Hotel of Sct Thomas is located in a residential area, a stone throw away from Copenhagen's culinary hotspot, parks and the hip bars of Vesterbro.

Although the rooms are rather small, they are tastefully decorated. Being in a residential area, the hotel guarantees its guests a peaceful night's sleep. The rate of their double rooms starts at £78.

Address: Frederiksberg Alle 7, 1621
Phone:+45 3321 6464
Hotel Sct Thomas Website
http://www.hotelsctthomas.dk/
Hotel Sct Thomas Map
https://goo.gl/maps/uLbP3kifEJA2

Tivoli Hotel
This is a newly established hotel meant to accommodate the visitors of the theme park, Tivoli Gardens. The hotel may not share the same historical charm that the 168-year old theme park boasts of but Tivoli Hotel does feature some classic elements borrowed from the park.

Aside from the basic modern amenities, Tivoli Hotel offers various entertainment options for their guests. They have a pool and both indoor and outdoor play area which makes the hotel ideal for families. They have special deals for vacationing families too. The rate for double rooms starts at £110 which already includes entry fee to the Tivoli Gardens.

Address: Arni Magnussons Gade 2, 1577
Phone:+45 4487 0000
Tivoli Hotel Website
http://www.tivolihotel.dk/

Tivoli Hotel Map
https://goo.gl/maps/PsyfNxjaC272

Ibsens Hotel

Found near the shopping street of Nansensgade, Ibsens has a charming location. It is sandwiched between the lakes that surround the city center and the downtown area. It is also a short walk away from the Nørreport train station which has routes going northbound the coastline that leads to Louisiana art museum and a connection to Sweden as well.

The hotel has a vintage feel to it. The design is very much inspired by local art and fashion. In addition to its charming and convenient location, Ibsens is quite affordable as well. The double rooms start at £100.

Address: Vendersgade 23, 1363
Phone:+45 3313 1913
Ibsens Hotel Website
http://www.arthurhotels.dk/ibsens-hotel/
Ibsens Hotel Map
https://goo.gl/maps/GMYxrdMJeZA2

11

Restaurants

Copenhagen attracts thousands of visitors from all over the world each year not only for their charming streets, lively events and rich art and history. Copenhagen is also known as a culinary hotspot. Do not miss out a unique gastronomic experience during your trip. Check out these delightful restaurants.

Madklubben Vesterbro
Found in the hip Vesterbro area, Madklubben has a wide range of menu. This restaurant is hard to miss because of its unique facade that looks like a transistor radio. They serve everything here from risotto to steak. They have classic Danish cuisines and international dishes. Customers can even put together their own menu. One-course meal is priced around DKK 100. Two-course meals are at DKK 150, three-course meals are at DKK 200 and four-course meals are at DKK 250.

Madklubben is known all over Copenhagen as a mid-budget restaurant with an intimate atmosphere that serves quality food. The restaurant is open daily between 5:30pm and 12mn on October to December.

Address: Vesterbrogade 62, 1620 København V
Phone: +45 3841 4143

Madklubben Vesterbro Website
http://madklubben.dk/en/
Madklubben Vesterbro Map
https://goo.gl/maps/UpkqwHMT4pG2

Geist

Danish celebrities rave about this cool restaurant. Owned by Chef Bo Bech, Geist serves tasty and well composed dishes. The most recommended from the menu is the mashed potato with brown stone crab and salted butter. Guests can also create their own menu by choosing two or three savory dishes paired with a sweet dish.

Geist looks like a high end restaurant but it is not as expensive as one might think. A dish can cost around DKK 81 to DKK 237. After the meal, have some coffee and sweet cotton candy. And after a sumptuous dinner, walk by the water at Nyhavn or take a boat tour.

Address: Kongens nytorv 8, 1050 København K
Phone: +45 33 13 37 13
Geist Website
http://restaurantgeist.dk/en/
Geist Map
https://goo.gl/maps/Mi1E8MVnLzp

Marv & Ben

Found along the charming medieval cobblestone street of Snaregade, Marv & Ben is classified as a Bib Gourmand restaurant but prides itself as a gastro pub. They serve modern Danish cuisine. Their ingredients are fresh and local. In fact, the restaurant has its own garden. There are no complications in their menu. The dishes are unpretentious but ultimately flavorful.

Marv & Ben's menu changes from season to season to ensure

optimum freshness in their ingredients. They are open on Tuesdays to Saturdays between 6pm and 12mn all year round. The price for two-course meals starts at DKK 325.

<u>Address:</u> Snaregade 4, 1205 København K
<u>Phone:</u> +45 3391 0191
Marv & Ben Website
http://cargocollective.com/marvogben
Marv & Ben Map
https://goo.gl/maps/6oN1UeBhyuT2

Cofoco Restaurant

This popular restaurant is found at the Vesterbro district. Cofoco stands for Copenhagen Food Consulting. Restaurant Cofoco is a favorite among menu because of their quality food offered at reasonable prices. The interior is designed according to contemporary style. Their trendy seating arrangements are quite comfortable. The price for their four-course meals is around DKK 275. The restaurant is open daily between 5:30pm and 12mn from October to December.

<u>Address:</u> Abel Cathrines Gade 7, 1650 København V
<u>Phone:</u> +45 3313 6060
Cofoco Restaurant Website
http://cofoco.dk/
Cofoco Restaurant Map
https://goo.gl/maps/6zk9mjn156w

Höst

Part of the Cofoco restaurant chain, Höst is found in the Nansensgade area near the lakes. The restaurant serves fine Nordic food at affordable prices. Their top rated dishes include the beef, lobster and Danish cheese hailed from the North Sea Coast.

The charming rooms are beautifully decorated in raw style. They use zinc, concrete, granite and recycled wood for the furnishings. Their benches and chairs are adorned with lambskin and plaids. Three-course meals start at DKK 295. Höst is open daily between 5:30pm and 12mn from October to December.

Address: Nørre Farimagsgade 41, 1364 København K
Phone: +45 8993 8409
Höst Website
https://www.facebook.com/restauranthoest/
Höst Map
https://goo.gl/maps/GUxkxAEpWv52

12

Special Things to Do only in Copenhagen

Here's a list of unique experiences you can only have in this great city.

Check out the Frederiksborg Palace north of Copenhagen.

There's nothing quite like it. Surrounded by a lake and a beautiful garden, the construction of the Frederiksborg Palace began in the 1600s under King Christian IV. Stroll down the romantic Palace Garden.

Address: Møntportvejen 10, 3400 Hillerød
Frederiksborg Palace Website
http://www.dnm.dk/UK/Forside.htm
Frederiksborg Palace Map
https://goo.gl/maps/D42BJE7eheA2

Explore the Freetown Christiania.
Discover an alternative way of life by the inhabitants of this free town. Check out the homemade houses, organic eateries, art galleries and green neighborhood. Before entering Christiana, you will find a list of 'do's and don'ts' abide by these rules.

Copenhagen's green and car-free neighborhood
Among the things worth checking out are the Christiana Blacksmith,

the Christiana Cykler, the Grey Hall, the Gay House and Morgenstedet. You can also have lunch at Spiseloppen.

Enjoy the beauty of nature at the Botanical Garden.
Enjoy the peace and stillness at the 10-hectare garden. Check out the historical glass houses. There are 27 of them. Among the most visited is the one at the Palm House built in 1874. It stands 16 meters tall. The passageway to the top is paved by cast-iron spiral stairs.

Address: Øster Farimagsgade 2B, 1353 København K
Phone: +45 3532 2222
Freetown Christiania Map
https://goo.gl/maps/2AmuRWVXSnN2

Discover something new at the Experimentarium City.
It's going to be a fun and interesting tour especially for kids and the kids at heart. Experience science in action and in all its forms; satisfy your curiosity and enjoy the outdoor activities.

Experimentarium city is also a good place for a waterfront view of The Opera, The Royal Danish Playhouse and the Nyhavn. You can also enjoy some of the best street foods Copenhagen has to offer in this location.

Address: Trangravsvej 10-12, 1436 København K
Phone: +45 3927 3333
Experimentarium City Website
http://en.experimentarium.dk/
Experimentarium City Map
https://goo.gl/maps/hiFBvUHsp2A2

Observe at The Round Tower.
This is Europe's oldest functioning observatory built in the 17th

century. Discover why the tower has made great astronomical achievements. See it for yourself. The Round Tower also houses a library hall where H.C. Andersen used to visit. There is also a glass floor where visitors can stand in and see the tower's core.

Address: Købmagergade 52A, 1150 København K
Phone: +45 3373 0373
Observe at The Round Tower Website
http://www.rundetaarn.dk/en/
Observe at The Round Tower Map
https://goo.gl/maps/NR8tQGjUmcs

Visit Carlsberg.
Your trip to Copenhagen won't be complete without a visit to this world famous brewery. Find out how Carlsberg makes their beer. Visitors can even sample Carlsberg products while enjoying a view

of the copper vessels.

Address: Gamle Carlsberg vej 11, 1799 København V
Phone: +45 3327 1282
Carlsberg Website
http://www.visitcarlsberg.dk/
Carlsberg Map
https://goo.gl/maps/CMEzAU34ZwT2

Amalienborg Palace

If you have extra time in Copenhagen, then be sure to go and see the changing of the guards at the royal palace.London(UK) is not the only country in Europe with a Royal family and a changing of the guards.Amalienborg is the home of the Danish Royal family.The Royal Guards march from Rosenborg Castle(11:30 am) to Amalienborg Palace(12:00 pm).The changing of the guards ceremony starts at Amalienborg Palace at 12 pm every day.

Phone: +45 33 12 21 86
Address: Amalienborg Slotsplads 5, 1257 København K
Amalienborg Website
http://www.kongernessamling.dk/en/amalienborg/palacesquare/
Amalienborg Map
https://goo.gl/maps/AMUjrGuwhkF2

13

3-Day Itinerary

Day One – Copenhagen
6:30am Breakfast at the hotel

9:00am Begin your tour at the bronze statue of the spinner of fairy tales, Hans Christian Andersen at the Town Hall Square or Rådhuspladsen.

9:30am Walk along the 18th century houses at Lavendelstræde and see where Mozart and Constanze used to live

10:00am Walk along Slutterigade to see the city's law courts which used to be town hall built in 1805 and 1815

10:30am Walk past the 19th century houses at Nytorv

11:00am Check out Copenhagen's shopping district at Strøget

12:30 pm Lunch Break

1:30pm Continue the tour at Copenhagen's Oldest Church, Helligåndskirken, built in the 15th century

2:00pm Check out Christian IV's bronze replica of the 1688 sculpture at Kongens Nytorv

2:20pm Stop by for pictures at the Nikolaj Kirke from the 1530s.

2:40pm Visit the equestrian statue of Copenhagen's founder, Bishop Absalon at the Højbro Plads where you can also enjoy a stunning view of the Thorvaldsens Museum on Slotsholmen.

3:10pm Enjoy a panoramic view of the Christiansborg Palace from the Gammel Strand.

3:30pm Check out the old fashioned street of Snaregade.

4:00pm See the oldest structures in Copenhagen at the Magstræde, dating back to the 16th century.

4:30pm Head to the Tivoli Gardens. Check out the cafés and beer gardens there.

7:00pm Dinner at Geist

9:00pm Boat tour by the canal

Day Two
6:30am Breakfast at the hotel

9:00am Start at the "King's New Market" or Kongens Nytorv. Check out the Magasin, Copenhagen's biggest department store.

9:20am See the Thott's Mansion, originally built for a Danish naval hero, now houses the French Embassy.

9:40am Visit the Royal Theatre founded in 1748.

10:00am Take pictures at the baroque style building of Charlottenborg Palace.

10:20am Check out Frederik V's statue and the residence of the queen and prince at the Amalienborg Palace.

10:40am Enjoy the view of the waterfront gardens at Amaliehavn.

11:10am Check out the marble church at Frederikskirke built in 1740.

11:30am Pay your respects to The Little Mermaid, the symbol of Copenhagen, near Den Lille Havfrue.

12:00nn Visit Amalienborg Palace for the changing of the guards.

1:30pm Check out where Hans Christian Andersen lived at no. 18, 20 and 67 at Nyhavn.

2:00pm Visit The Museum of National History.

3:30pm Head to Glyptoteket.

5:00pm Stop by for a quick bite at Café Glyptoteket.

6:30pm Visit The National Gallery of Denmark.

8:00pm Dinner at a Copenhagen restaurant of your choice.

10:30pm Check out one of the beer pubs or nightclubs.

Day Three
6:30am Breakfast at the hotel

9:00am Explore Christiana

11:00am Early Lunch

12:30pm Check out The Round Tower

1:30pm Visit the Botanical Garden

2:30pm Visit Carlsberg

5:00pm Go on a Shopping Spree

7:00pm Dinner at a restaurant of your choice

14

Conclusion

I want to thank you for reading this book! I sincerely hope that you received value from it!

If you received value from this book, I want to ask you for a favour. Would you be kind enough to leave a review for this book on Amazon?

Please Click Here to Review This Book on Amazon.com

CHECK OUT MY OTHER BOOKS!!

https://www.amazon.com/Helsinki-Best-Short-Travel-Guides-ebook/dp/B01HLA41EC/

https://www.amazon.com/Prague-Short-Travel-Republic-Guides-ebook/dp/B015T8FZVG/

http://shortstaytravel.com/author-books/

Ó Copyright 2016 by Gary Jones - All rights reserved.

This document is geared towards providing exact and reliable information in regards to the topic and issue covered. The publication is sold with the idea that the publisher is not required to render accounting, officially permitted, or otherwise, qualified services. If advice is necessary, legal or professional, a practiced individual in the profession should be ordered.

- From a Declaration of Principles which was accepted and approved equally by a Committee of the American Bar Association and a Committee of Publishers and Associations.

In no way is it legal to reproduce, duplicate, or transmit any part of this document in either electronic means or in printed format. Recording of this publication is strictly prohibited and any storage of this document is not allowed unless with written permission from the publisher. All rights reserved.

The information provided herein is stated to be truthful and consistent, in that any liability, in terms of inattention or otherwise, by any usage or abuse of any policies, processes, or directions contained within is the solitary and utter responsibility of the recipient reader. Under no circumstances will any legal responsibility or blame be held against the publisher for any reparation, damages, or monetary loss

CONCLUSION

due to the information herein, either directly or indirectly.

Respective authors own all copyrights not held by the publisher.

The information herein is offered for informational purposes solely, and is universal as so. The presentation of the information is without contract or any type of guarantee assurance.

The trademarks that are used are without any consent, and the publication of the trademark is without permission or backing by the trademark owner. All trademarks and brands within this book are for clarifying purposes only and are the owned by the owners themselves, not affiliated with this document.

Made in United States
Troutdale, OR
02/15/2024